ISBN 978-0-331-43124-7
PIBN 11122943

Historic, archived document

Do not assume content reflects current
scientific knowledge, policies, or practices.

EVALUATION PLANNER
FOR EXTENSION

FOR EXTENSION

UNITED STATES
DEPARTMENT OF
AGRICULTURE

EXTENSION
SERVICE

ESC- 585

<u>FOREWORD</u>

Evaluation is currently one of the more popular topics in Extension. Underlying this concern for evaluation is the basic concept of accountability. This is in part due to an emphasis or a demand to be accountable for the organizational resources utilized in conducting Extension's educational programs. Another reason is the desire to know what difference a program has made in the lives of people involved in Extension programs.

Much has been said and written about evaluation and the references are many. There is considerable interest in the "how-to-conduct" an evaluation. This is one of the major reasons for the <u>Evaluation Planner</u>. The <u>Planner</u> is an attempt to assist an Extension worker in planning and organizing the evaluation process. It is an aid to thinking through what needs to be considered--the purpose, organization, and conduct of an evaluation. It deals with the "Who, What, When, Where, Why, and How" of evaluation, and is intended for use at any of the different levels in the Extension organization.

The <u>Planner</u> is intended as an aid in structuring an evaluation and should be helpful for those who have little or even much experience in conducting an evaluation. It is an attempt to provide useful information and serve as a guide for those who have a need for practical evaluation resource material. The real value of the <u>Planner</u> will be in its application by those interested in conducting an evaluation but who have limited time and resources.

The <u>Planner</u> includes a list of references for those who wish to explore the subject of evaluation more extensively. A glossary lists terms commonly used in the area of evaluation. Further, the <u>Planner</u> has been developed around, and incorporates, the basic concepts of Extension's program development process.

Evaluation is a broad subject and could not be covered extensively in any one book. The author, John Gross, has provided a helpful overview of and a practical approach to the subject, drawing on his own experience in the field.

E. RICHARD WHEATON
Program & Staff Development
Extension Service
U.S. Department of Agriculture

TABLE OF CONTENTS

EVALUATION PLANNER

for

Extension

By John G. Gross,
Extension Studies Specialist
University of Missouri

'Evaluation, a dimension of the program development process,
deals with judgments or decisionmaking. Many decisions must be
made from the inception to the completion of an Extension program.

This Evaluation Planner can help make these decisions easier
for you. It can serve as a time-saver and memory-jogger--a practical
guide to call attention to some of the points you should consider in
program evaluation.. It is not intended to be an exhaustive resource
on evaluation; many good texts on that subject are listed in the
References section' at the end of this publication.

This Evaluation Planner is based on the "Evaluation Planning
Sheet" (page 8). The planning sheet lists factors such as "decision-
situation," "purpose," "audience," etc., that should be considered
in planning an evaluation study. Corresponding chapters in this
Evaluation Planner elaborate on each of these factors. The same
factors apply whether you are evaluating one meeting or a
comprehensive long-term program.

The Planner will not do the evaluation for you, but it will
help you think through and organize your evaluation process.

EVALUATION AS A CONCEPT

Evaluation is a difficult, yet necessary, part of Extension educational programs. Few Extension directors, specialists and program leaders are satisfied with only the subjective judgments of program accomplishments. As a result, some have turned to more scientific methods of educational research. Evaluation, because of the many human elements involved, probably is destined to remain a more highly complex judgmental process than a research process. Evaluation, as used here, means to examine or judge in order to determine the value of an educational program.

Everyday judgments and opinions play some part in decision-making. However, evaluation involves decisionmaking based upon information that has been systematically gathered, examined, and applied to some standards or criteria.

Evaluation must not be equated with research, though many similarities can be found. In its broadest sense, research includes evaluation, and evaluation may use some research procedures and fact-finding methods. However, evaluation and research differ in purpose and, to some degree, in method.

The aim of research is to develop new knowledge. New knowledge may not be immediately applicable for practical use. The goal of program evaluation is to provide information for enlightened decisionmaking to help establish or improve programs. The use of control groups, the selection of matched groups of participants, and other experimental research methods are not necessarily required for evaluations designed to provide value judgments.

Educational Program Evaluation

Each Extension program should have specified educational objectives. Generally, the aim of Extension is to bring about educational change in the learners, and through them, to favorably affect other individuals and groups, the secondary consumers of Extension educational services.

Evaluation, by discovering and measuring the effectiveness of programs, projects, methods, and materials used in an educational Extension program, directly contributes to improvement not only of the educational process but also to Extension programs provided to communities.

One educator defines this type of evaluation as "enlightenment for decisionmaking."

4

Evaluation as a Continuing Process

Evaluation begins before an educational program is planned. Once the need or opportunity for change has been decided upon, a series of prejudgments based upon knowledge and experience contribute to the decisions about what educational objectives, materials and methods are to be used.

Information collected formally, or sometimes informally, before and during a program provides the input for periodic evaluations of the program's progress. Data gathered and analyzed when the program ends, along with that gathered and analyzed previously, serves as the basis for decisions about continuing or changing the educational program.

In this manner, evaluation becomes a continuous, active, circular process in which the results are put into practical use as soon as they are determined.

Value judgments necessarily play a large part in educational evaluation because control over variables--essential to research-- may not be possible. Some techniques of testing and measurement used in research, however, are at times practical and applicable in the evaluation process.

Evaluation--Long-Range and Immediate

Long-Range Outcome Evaluation: In the broadest sense each program can be judged for its contribution in the effort to solve identified problems of people, families, and communities.

In a narrower sense, a program may be evaluated in terms of its effect upon the participants. How did the educational program influence them to change and how has, or will, this in turn affect their families and communities?

This kind of long-range outcome evaluation is difficult. Community studies, or broad-range attitude studies, are often difficult and expensive. Frequently estimates must serve. However, when expert resources are available, some of the most tangible and useful evaluations will measure the outcome in terms of improved indices of change.

Immediate Operational Evaluation: A continuing education program may also be evaluated as a process. How efficiently and effectively did it function while seeking to accomplish its results?

Upon completion of all or portion of a program, it may be evaluated against one or more of its specific objectives. For example, if the program was designed to impart a given body of knowledge to a given number of participants in a specified amount of time, this can be measured.

With a little planning, several types of data useful in operational or process evaluation can be gathered in advance of, during, and following the program. (1) Cost data and enrollment data will give the background for evaluating the effectiveness in terms of the cost per participant reached. (2) Participant achievement records will provide a basis for evaluating whether the program has achieved some of its more specifically stated educational objectives. (3) "Happiness data" (formally and informally gathered opinions of the participants and faculty) will give a reading on whether the participants received what they expected.

The Elements of Evaluation

WHO should be interested in Extension program evaluation?

Anyone who makes decisions about Extension programs. These may be decisions about what should be the objectives, strategies to use, or assessing the program impact. Therefore, everyone who makes decisions about Extension programs has an interest in Extension program evaluation.

WHAT is evaluation? Evaluation may have many different meanings. For the purposes of this "Planner," evaluation is making judgments and decisions based on information. It includes the process of specifying, obtaining, and interpreting data to give meaningful information for judgments and decision-making about Extension programs.

Evaluation is an important dimension of the program development process. Evaluation should not be thought of as a separate concept, but as a phase of program development--that phase which involves the making of decisions and judgments. It is a process in which evidence and criteria are provided to serve as a rational basis for judgments and decisions.

WHEN should a systematic evaluation be planned? Evaluation goes on all the time and everywhere decisions are made. The issue is, how formal and deliberate should the evaluation effort be? This depends on the confidence the program planner has in his decisionmaking ability. Certain decisions may have to be based on "hard" data.[1] When the program developer decides that the quality of evidence used in decision situations should be "hard" versus "soft" data, then a systematic evaluation is called for. The degree of "hardness" of data selected depends on a trade-off between ideal data for the evaluative purpose at hand and the resources available. The "hard" data are more expensive and difficult to obtain, and should be collected when the benefits to decisionmaking from this superior evidence will outweigh the cost of obtaining such evidence.[2]

---

[1]Claude Bennett, Analyzing Impacts of Extension Programs (Extension Service, USDA, ESC575, Washington, D.C.), pp. 11-13.

[2]Op cit. Bennett, p. 11.

WHERE should evaluation be done? Evaluation should be done at the level at which the decision is to be made. Evaluation of local programs should be made locally.

WHY should Extension spend extra effort on systematic evaluation? There is increased emphasis on evaluation and accountability.[3] Accountability can be demonstrated through evaluation, and evaluation efforts are needed to meet these accountability demands.

HOW can you carry out an evaluation systematically? That's what this publication is about. On the following page is the "Evaluation Planning Sheet" which outlines a procedure that can assist you in conducting many evaluation efforts.

---

[3] USDA Secretary's Memorandum No. 1777, dated April 6, 1972, and Secretary's Memorandum No. 1777 Supplement 1, dated August 22, 1972.

EVALUATION PLANNING SHEET

Reference
Page

DECISION
SITUATION: What category of evaluation will be conducted?

Determination (Situation) (Ref. p.25)	Strategy (Plan of Work) (Ref. p.30)	Action (Implementation) (Ref. p.40)	Product (Accomplishments) (Ref. p.49)

PURPOSE: What will the evaluation achieve?   11

AUDIENCE: Who is the evaluation for?   13

ISSUES: What do you want to find out?   14

EVIDENCE: What information will be needed?   15

DATA GATHERING: How will information be collected?   16

    a. Instrument: What questions will be asked
       to get information?

    b. From whom: source of information--sampling.

    c. Time schedule: When:

    d. Information to be collected by whom?

ANALYSIS: What does the data mean?   17

    a. Instructions for editing, coding, and
       tabulating.

    b. Relationships and comparisons to be made.

    c. Statistical analysis to be used.

    d. Analysis and interpretation to be done
       by whom? When?

    e. Conclusion and recommendations to be
       developed by whom?

REPORTING: How can the evaluation findings be reported?   18

    a. Means of presenting the findings.

    b. Format of the report.

    c. Date for reporting the findings.

RESOURCES: a. Personnel requirements: staff time.   19

    b. Budget: money.

HOW TO USE THE PLANNER

There are numerous decisions that must be made from the inception to the completion of an Extension program. This planner is to provide help in these decision situations. The story is told of an army recruit who was given the job of sorting potatoes. When asked how he liked his job, he replied, "The job isn't so bad, it's just making the decisions!" Likewise, in Extension, the making of decisions is the difficult task. This document is devised to make this decision-making task easier.

The program development process has been identified as consisting of six processes. The first two of these--developing an institutional framework and developing an organizational base--are preliminary and preparatory processes of program development. The making of decisions and judgments is clustered into the remaining four processes--program determination (situation), program strategy (plan of work), program action (implementation), and program evaluation (accomplishments).[4]

The Evaluation Planner for Extension is a guide to the evaluation process. It will serve as a time saver and memory jogger--to call attention to some things that should be considered in planning an evaluation. The Planner will be a resource and help. It is not an exhaustive resource on evaluation, but is a practical guide. A reference list is included for more detailed information.

The Planner is summarized in the "Evaluation Planning Sheet." Following is a brief discussion of the uses of the "Planning Sheet." An evaluation can be summarized on this sheet (or with as many additional sheets as required). The planning sheet gives a logical process to follow in planning evaluations:

DECISION SITUATION--(What category* of evaluation will be conducted, and what decisions or judgments must be made about the program?) These evaluation decisions occur throughout the program development process. At these points, the evaluator should identify the kinds of judgments or decisions of greatest concern, such as:

. Determination of objectives
. Plan of work strategy
. Program implementation
. Accomplishment

A summary of relationships among the four categories of evaluations, the program development components, and decision situations, is shown in Appendix Table 1.

---

[4] Extension Program Development, by Program Development Ad Hoc Committee, Roger L. Lawrence, Chairman (Ames, Iowa, 1973), pp. 4-5.

*Refer to Planning Sheet, p. 8.

After this first step--defining the situation--we may identify and follow eight more steps in the evaluation process. The first four of these involve the planning and design of evaluation, the last four, the methodology and procedure of the evaluation.

PURPOSE--(What is to be achieved by doing the evaluation?) You must be clear about what you want from an evaluation. Is it worth the effort?* (11)**

AUDIENCE--(Who is the evaluation for?) This determines your approach. Is it for the staff, the supervisors, or external audiences? Who will be interested in the results of the evaluation? (13)

ISSUES--(What do you want to find out?) Be specific about the things to be examined. You can't consider everything about a program but must identify the most significant and relevant issues. (14)

EVIDENCE--(What information will be needed?) When the issues have been identified, the next step is to determine what data will be needed to answer questions pertinent to the issues. What questions will have to be asked to obtain the needed information? (15)

> The remainder of the Evaluation Planning Sheet refers to collecting, handling and interpreting data so that the needed information will emerge.

DATA GATHERING--(How will the information be collected?) Will it be by interview, mailed survey, telephone, etc.? The evaluator must determine what questions to ask, who to get the information from, and the time schedule. Decide who is going to collect the information, and when. (16)

ANALYSIS--(What do the data mean?) Raw data itself may not have much meaning. The comparisons and relationships among the data must be specified so that meaning will emerge. Who will analyze and interpret the data? Who will develop the conclusions and recommendations? (17)

REPORTING--(How can the evaluation findings be reported?) How will the audience be informed of the findings? When? What means of presentation will be used? (18)

RESOURCES--Every study will require staff time and perhaps money. The amount will depend on the comprehensiveness and depth of the study. (19)

---

*Refer to pages 20-60 for a detailed description of each category of evaluation.
**This number refers to the page where this step in the evaluation process is discussed.

PURPOSE: WHY EVALUATE?

All Extension workers do some kind of evaluation in their day-to-day work. They make decisions, draw conclusions, and form judgments. Evaluation is not concerned primarily with knowledge for knowledge's sake, but with knowledge for action. Evaluation is concerned more with decisions in a specific setting than with making broad generalizations.

Evaluation is done by people related to a program. These people are the ones involved in and affected by the things Extension does. Extension program personnel take the lead in systematic evaluation efforts. A few Extension programs have used outside evaluators to gather, analyze, and interpret evaluative data.

There is an increasing tendency for evaluation to be formally included in educational program proposals. Resources for evaluation may vary, but there is an increased need for program accountability. Carl N. Scheneman, Vice-president for Extension, University of Missouri, stated, "During the past 5 years we have been asked more and more for accountability--from the governor's office, from legislators, county judges, and even University administrators."[5]

Better quality data used in decisionmaking will contribute to better decisions. Better decisions made in the course of program planning and implementation will result in better programs.

Evaluation can serve the purposes of program planning, policy making, program improvement, program justification, and accountability. Evaluation may also serve as a basis for program publicity, contribute to staff improvement and development, and provide documentation about the history and impact of a program.

Educational evaluation is more than assessing what happened to the "student" as a result of the program. It includes the gathering, analysis, and use of data to provide information about the nature and worth of educational programs in order to improve decisions about the management of those programs.

Careful planning of an evaluation is important. Some things to consider in this planning are:

1. Can you clearly and explicitly state the goals of the evaluation study?

2. Do these goals describe an effort that is worth doing?

---

[5]Carl N. Scheneman, "Remarks to University of Missouri Statewide Staff Meeting, October 13, 1976," Exclaimer, Vol. 4 No. 6, (Nov.-Dec. 1976).

3. Are you familiar with the characteristics of those persons from whom you will request information?

4. Have you estimated the costs of the evaluation in terms of both time and money? It is easy to underestimate these.

The audience for an evaluation, the issues considered, and the analysis of the data will affect the purposes for the evaluation.

Perhaps a short summary of purpose would be, "It is well to know what you intend to accomplish before you do it."

AUDIENCE: WHO IS THE EVALUATION FOR?

Who has a primary interest in the results of an evaluation? Who will be making the decisions and judgments based on the findings of a systematic evaluation study? Are there other interested parties that have a right to the evaluative information?

Usually, an evaluation focuses on one main audience. Audiences and their information requirements vary. The information needs of the county director, for instance, may differ from those of the advisory board for the program. The county director may be more concerned with efficiency while the advisory committee may be more concerned with program impact.

Selecting your main audience influences the questions to be addressed by the evaluation and is related to the purpose to be achieved by doing the evaluation.

An evaluation cannot be 'all things to all audiences." The evaluation should collect data to provide information specific to the requirements of the particular audience for the evaluation. It should take into account their expectations of the evaluation and the program, the criteria or standards by which they will judge the program success, indicators of program performance they look for, and the forms of reporting they find most useful.

The work of analyzing, selecting, and digesting should be done by the evaluator--not the audience. Churchill, responsible for the British Empire's war effort in World War II, insisted on one-page reports. "...if Churchill could get adequate reports on one page each, what business executive could not, with advantage, make similar demands of his staff?"[6] Extension personnel could take note of this in their reports. Our evaluations should give specific information to the audience that needs it.

---

[6] Royal Bank of Canada Monthly Letter, Vol. 57, No. 9 (Montreal, September 1976), p. 4.

ISSUES: WHAT DO YOU WANT TO FIND OUT?

The evaluator must identify the concerns and questions of the audience about the program. In order to make the evaluation effort useful and meaningful, the evaluator must decide on the issues. The issues must relate to the needs, problems, and interests of the audience.

Both audience and issues determine the questions to be asked. Data gathered in answer to these questions provide information for making decisions and judgments about the program.

If all issues cannot be addressed with available resources, assign priorities on which issues to include in the evaluation.

Specific issues that provide the basis for evaluation questions include:

. Evidence of program outcomes

. Accountability for program processes and costs

. The extent to which needs were addressed

. Whether or not goals were fulfilled

. Whether or not program promises were kept.

Criteria for selecting issues for program evaluation include practical considerations such as:[7]

. Can the results of an evaluation influence decisions regarding a program?

. Can the evaluation be completed in time to be helpful to decisionmakers?

. Can the evaluation be done? Is sufficient data obtainable on the important effects of the program?

. Can sufficient resources be obtained to meet the time schedule and technical requirements of the evaluation?

. Has the program been stable enough so that an evaluation will provide relevant information?

. Is the program significant enough to merit the evaluation effort?

---

[7]Harry Hatry, Richard Winnie, and Donald Fisk, Practical Program Evaluation for State and Local Government Officials, (The Urban Institute, Washington, D.C., 1973), p. 110.

EVIDENCE: WHAT EVIDENCE SHOULD BE COLLECTED?

Evaluation efforts deal with selected issues. Once issues are selected, the search for evidence begins. Evidence is information that contributes to the consideration of an issue addressed by an evaluation. Decisions and judgments about a program should be made on the basis of high quality evidence.

Evidence may take many forms: descriptions of program activities and outcomes; statements about the value of the program, collected from various people; speculations about causes and effects of program successes. Different kinds of issues and audiences require different kinds of evidence.

The quality of the evidence can be assessed by considering:

. The relevance of the data to the issues and audiences.

. The balance and scope of the evidence.

. The degree to which the data gathering instrument measures the objectives it is supposed to measure (validity).

. The consistency of the responses making up the data (reliability).

. Assessing the degree to which the claimed outcomes are due to the program rather than to other factors.

. The degree to which side effects and other unanticipated outcomes have been identified.

. The degree to which the evidence is believable.

A useful rule of thumb is to select and collect only data needed to assess the issues in question. The evaluator should forego the temptation to collect data that would be "nice to know," and be concerned with data needed to serve as evidence.

Data should not be used just because it is available. Selection of data for evidence depends upon its descriptive or judgmental value, its power as evidence, and its cost.

DATA GATHERING: HOW IS THE EVIDENCE TO BE COLLECTED?

After deciding on the kind of evidence needed, the evaluator should decide on the amount of data to collect, and from which sources. Data sources are the people or things that provide evidence about the program.

In gathering data, consider:

. the proportion and representativeness of the data sources
   to be used (sampling procedures)

. ethical questions (invasion of privacy)

. treatment and interpretation of the data

. constraints imposed by limitations of resources.

Data gathering strategies must be considered. Think about the appropriateness of data gathering techniques (questionnaires, interviews, direct observations, etc.) Some means of data gathering are more obtrusive on program operation than others.

Existing instruments may be available and apply to an evaluation need. Or, the evaluator may need to develop, modify or adapt unique instruments or procedures to the evaluation effort.

In selecting or developing a questionnaire, note whether the questions:

. Ask for only one bit of information
. Use wording that implies a desired answer
. Use words with double meanings that may cause misunder-
   standing
. Contain words unfamiliar to the respondents
. Use words emotionally loaded, vaguely defined, or overly
   ·general
. Relate to some purpose of the study
. Follow a logical order or sequence.

Consider the timing of data collection, explanations to people about the reasons for collecting certain data, and the appropriate means for processing and handling the data.

ANALYSIS: HOW CAN THE EVIDENCE BY ANALYZED?

Once the data have been gathered, they must be analyzed in order to determine what they say about the program. It is important to order and analyze the data so that answers will be provided for the issues in question. It is important that the analysis be performed on relevant, high quality data. Sophisticated analysis performed on inadequate or inappropriate data may lead to false implications and conclusions. It is important for the analysis to be applicable to the audience concerned.

Good data analysis will help evaluate descriptions of the program. Such analysis may describe a program during a given time period, or document change over time. Comparisons might be made with current and previous program impacts, processes, or outcomes, or with similar aspects of other programs.

There are many ways to analyze evaluation data. The choice of an analysis technique will depend on the nature of the information to be analyzed, the purpose of the analysis, and the resources available.

Usually, the type of data analysis is linked to the type of evidence, the concerns of the audiences, and to their ability to understand the information.

REPORTING: HOW CAN EVALUATION FINDINGS BE REPORTED?

The payoff of an evaluation effort comes when the findings
are reported (or communicated) to the intended audience. The
report must be presented in such a way that the findings are
organized according to the decisions and judgments to be made.
The selected questions should be answered by setting forth the
informative data answering to these questions. Interpretation may
be necessary as a part of the report. Implications and possible
alternatives may be suggested.

Keep the audience in mind when preparing the report. It
is important to understand the audience's criteria, standards and
indicators, and disseminate the findings that address those concerns
in language the audience will relate to and understand.

People have different abilities and experiences that influence
the way they receive and use evaluation reports. These differences
should be taken into account in reporting evaluation findings. Technical or statistical information may not be meaningful or under-
standable by some groups. Nontechnical, nonstatistical description
of program effectiveness, impact and functioning may sometimes be
more appropriate.

The evaluator must consider various reporting procedures.
The criteria for selection of the appropriate procedure is simple.
Use the procedure that best communicates the findings on the partic-
ular issues to your audience.

RESOURCES: WHAT RESOURCES ARE AVAILABLE FOR EVALUATION?

Before starting a major evaluation effort, the evaluator should know what resources are likely to be available. Knowing this in advance helps set the boundaries for the evaluation. As the evaluation design is developed, costs can be estimated and decisions made about the use of limited resources.

The evaluation plan should include cost estimates in terms of dollar outlay (e.g., supplies), time expenditure (e.g., interviews), and expertise needed (e.g., specialized persons). The plan should indicate how the evaluation will be managed and who will be responsible for each aspect of it.

When possible, use existing information that is regularly collected. New information may be needed, but may be costly to acquire.

Decisions about what percentage of program resources should be expended on evaluation cannot easily be made in advance. The investment in evaluation may be an investment in the future of the program. The amount of the investment will vary with the urgency of the accountability demands on the program and the value of reporting program performance. Reasonable costs can be decided by estimating the significance of the issues and the likely impact of the evaluation. However, various evaluation needs will entail different expenditure of resources. Some evaluation is possible within any budget.

CATEGORIES OF EVALUATION

The Extension program consists of agreed-upon priority needs, concerns, problems, and interests that fall within the scope of the Extension unit's responsibilities together with the objectives that are to be achieved within a designated period of time. Program development is the continuous series of processes involved in carrying out the Extension program. Evaluation, as defined in this "Planner," relates to making the decisions and judgments with the purpose of improving programs.

As we look at the schematic diagram (Figure 1, page 21) of Extension program development, there are four situations where decisions and judgments are critical. Decisions in program development tend to cluster into four processes.[8] These four processes are: Program Determination (Situation), Program Strategy (Plan of Work), Program Action (Implementation), and and Program Product (Accomplishments). These processes are discussed with examples in the chapter that follow.

Decision situations in Extension educational programs may be categorized as (1) program determination (situation), (2) program strategy (plan of work), (3) program action (implementation), and (4) program product (accomplishments). It also involves recycling decisions including decisions that call for termination, continuation or modification of program.

The evaluator must resolve a number of problems and sub-problems simultaneously. He needs to be able to define problems and refine and adjust solutions continuously. The development of solutions to problems is a delicate process of incorporating ideas into a viable operational situation. Usually these ideas are far from perfect and need to be improved periodically. Changes must be made whenever the evidence indicates that current program objectives are not being adequately met or may no longer be appropriate. Evaluation designs must allow for continuous adjustment and refinement.

Generally, evaluation involves providing information to serve as rational bases for making judgments in decision situations. To clarify this, it is helpful to define some key terms. A decision is a choice among alternatives. A decision situation is a set of alternatives. Judgment is the assigning of values to alternatives. A criterion is a rule or standard by which values are assigned to alternatives. Stated simply, evaluation is the science of using information for improved decisionmaking.

---

[8]Program Development Ad Hoc Committee, Roger Lawrence, Chairman, Extension Program Development, Iowa State University, Ames, Iowa, Aug. 1973, p. 5.

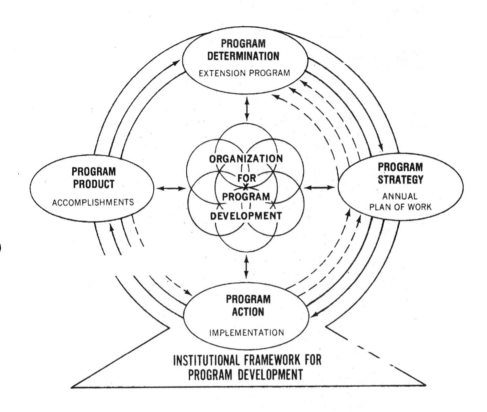

FIG.1 - PROCESSES OF EXTENSION PROGRAM DEVELOPMENT

Given the four broad categories of educational decisions to be served, there are then at least four categories of evaluation to be considered. These can be identified as (1) determination or situation evaluation (basic to program planning), (2) strategy evaluation (basic to plans of work), (3) program action or implementation evaluation, and (4) product or program accomplishment evaluation.

Determination or situation evaluation defines the environment or situation where change is to occur. It identifies people's unmet needs, problems underlying those needs, and opportunities for change. Information from determination evaluation is the basis for the establishment of program goals and objectives.

Strategy evaluation or plan of work evaluation determines resources needed, how to use them, and the mix of resources and methods to meet program goals and objectives. The object is to identify and assess relevant strategies, including resources needed to meet program goals. The end product of strategy evaluation is selection of a procedural design or the development of a plan of work that outlines accomplishments and potential benefits.

Program action or implementation evaluation provides periodic feedback to those concerned with the continuing control and refinement of plans and procedures. The object is to detect or predict strengths and weaknesses in the procedural or action design. This evaluation identifies and monitors potential sources of failure, such as logistics, communication channels, lack of understanding and acceptance of the program, inadequate resources, interpersonal relationships, and lack of staff resources such as competencies, time, and physical facilities.

Program product or accomplishment evaluation determines the accomplishments of the program or project during and after it has run its course. This cycle often needs to include the period of time necessary for expected changes to occur. The objective of product evaluation is to relate results to objectives and to determination, strategy, and program action evaluation information in order to measure and interpret accomplishments or product. This will help determine decisions on recycling, termination, continuation or modification of the program.

This four-step evaluation system is developed around the four critical decision situations in Cooperative Extension program development. The major objective of the system is to maximize the effectiveness of critical decisionmaking by reporting timely and relevant information in a useful form, and ultimately, optimizing the planning and conducting of educational programs. The system or model is designed to yield information to serve each of the four critical decision situations. Figure 2, page 23 is a conceptual model showing the relationship of these four categories of evaluation in sequence and to each other.

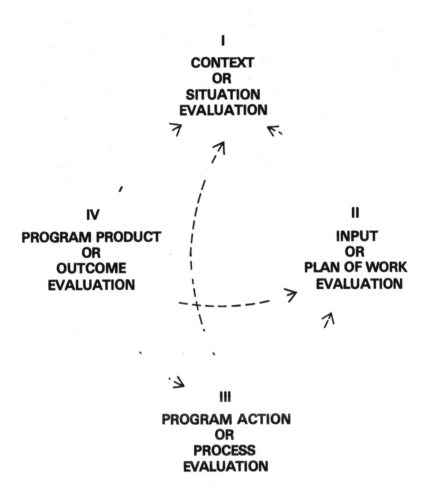

FIG. 2 - FOUR CATEGORIES OF EVALUATION FOR EDUCATIONAL PROGRAMS

A **key to** the effective operation of this model is that decisions are identified, along with the persons who are involved in the decision process, and that a systematic attempt is made to obtain relevant information in a usable form. However, the best information is useless if it is not available when needed. Therefore, another key to the operation of this evaluation model is to plan to have the best information ready for use when it is needed. Sometimes it is feasible to postpone making a decision, but often such a delay can be costly and/or impossible. The system must be geared to the time when critical decisions must be made so that it can produce the information in time for consideration.

The test of this evaluation model is the extent to which it (1) helps decisionmakers and evaluators understand the nature of the decisions they face, and (2) motivates them to have relevant and timely information available to aid in making those decisions.

PROGRAM DETERMINATION (SITUATION)

This is the stage of the program development process concerned with determining the organization and operational plan. The general situation is examined and analyzed to determine the relevant goals and priorities. The type of data and information collected at this stage is used to analyze and interpret concerns and problems. The problems and concerns to be included within Extension's scope and responsibility are determined. Priorities and objectives are set out.

The steps involved in a program determination evaluation study are:[9]

PURPOSE

The purpose of a program determination evaluation is to:

. Diagram and analyze problems
. Describe the relevant information
. Identify needed relationships with other agencies
. Identify unmet needs and unmet program opportunities
. Determine barriers and facilitators related to a program
. Set new boundaries for the program to be evaluated
. Look for new or emerging value orientations
. Provide a factual basis for public information
. Provide a basis for developing proposals for outside funding
. Establish benchmarks or current status of people and/or problems, for future planning.

AUDIENCE

The most common audiences for a program determination evaluation are: program and administrative staff, including Extension staff members, specialists, supervisors, program leaders, administrators, and directors.

In some instances, clientele groups such as advisory committees and councils, Extension councils, community or special interest groups or clientele organizations may be the audience. Less frequently, but possibly, funding bodies such as: county boards and commissions, state legislature, granting agencies, and Congress could be the audiences.

ISSUES

The program determination evaluation should address such issues as:

. What are the specific objectives?

---

[9]Reference: Evaluation Planning Sheet, page 8.

. What are current needs and clientele problems?

. What technological advances concern Extension?

. Can Extension cooperate with other agencies in implementing programs?

. What are the past effects of Extension in this area?

. Are there any opportunities for service within the scope of Extension?

. What are society's needs and values related to the program?

. Are there political trends to be considered?

. What local influences make a difference in the methods to be used?

. Are sufficient funds available for the program?

. What educational changes do the people want, individually or collectively?

EVIDENCE

Gathering data to provide necessary information to serve as evidence will involve decisions about:

. The data sources. Who will have the needed data?

. Sampling procedures. Will it be necessary to collect data from all of the data sources or could a sampling give adequate results? If so, how should the sample be selected? How large a sample should it be?

. Which questions to ask to get the needed information. The kinds of questions asked will depend upon the evidence needed to resolve the issues under consideration.

. Ethical questions such as invasion of privacy or other restraints.

. Techniques of data collection to be used. These may be mail questionnaires, interview schedules (personal or telephone), distributed questionnaires or checklists, group interviews, systematic observation, or other techniques. (See References.)

. Timing of the data gathering. Time must be available before setting out on a data gathering project.

ANALYSIS

Data collected must be analyzed for meaning, and ordered so that comparisons can be made to answer the questions raised in the concerned issues.

Evidence may result in a ranking or priority ordering so that answers to concerns can be logically determined. Analysis may involve comparison with similar programs.

REPORTING

The report will summarize the evaluation of the program determination effort. The progress and issues as evidenced will determine to a great extent the comprehensiveness of the report. It may be:

. Written or oral

. General or specific

. Technical or nontechnical

. Recommendation-making.

RESOURCES

Resources for program determination consist primarily of:

. staff time
. clerical help
. supplies
. volunteer help
. competencies of regular program staff
. organizational assistance provided.

Data resources include such records as:

. census data
. survey results
. reports from similar programs
. journal articles
. public hearings
. surveys
. SEMIS data.

In some cases, the availability of consultants, and outside operating help, and the availability of computer services may be considered.

EXAMPLE:* PROGRAM DETERMINATION EVALUATION

Family Farm Development Program

Beginning and developing farm families are faced with the problem of gaining control of sufficient resources to establish and maintain economical farm business units. They must make critical decisions concerning organization and growth when family foundation and development are highest.

Educational needs of developing farm families are great. They need an analysis of their situation, help to define problems, set objectives and an outline of a course of action.

PURPOSE

The purpose of the survey was to define a program that would reach farm families not participating or reached by either Extension's small farm program or the regular commercial agricultural program. The survey was designed to define the status of families, as a basis for further decisions on this type of programming.

AUDIENCE

The audience was the state farm family development committee and designated area Extension directors.

ISSUES

. What objectives should be sought?

. What areas of the state should be offered this program?

. What educational changes do the people want?

. What needs exist that Extension should be concerned about?

EVIDENCE

Information needed to resolve the issues at this stage of planning is available from agricultural, home economics and youth state program specialists.

The information to design a workable pilot program can be obtained from this group. As the program is planned and implemented, evidence will be needed from clientele and Extension field staff.

*This is an example intended only to illustrate the application of the planning sheet to an actual evaluation effort.

DATA GATHERING

Information was gathered at an agricultural program leaders' meeting. A committee was appointed to develop the proposal. Representatives of home economics and youth programs were included in the committee to draft the proposal for the program.

ANALYSIS

Program objectives were discussed and agreed upon by the farm family development program steering committee. A statistical analysis was not required.

Possible geographic areas were nominated as sites for the program. Contact with area Extension directors resulted in choosing five pilot areas for the program.

Criteria used to select areas to be invited to participate were:

. Number of full-time farmers with sales less than $20,000 in 1969 census.

. Number of young farm operators (less than 44 years of age in 1969 census).

. Importance of agriculture to the economy of the area.

. Interest of area director and area specialists.

. Potential for success in agriculture as a full-time family farm.

. Ratio of area staff to farm families and farm income.

. Acceptance and support by University Extension councils and influentials.

. Location in different counties than small farm program.

REPORTING

A proposal for approval and funding was presented to Vice-president for Extension in October, 1976.

RESOURCES

Available administrative funds were used to carry out the program and supplement field staff resource needs.

Six persons were employed for the program; 1 state staff and 5 field staff.

Other staff time and assignments shifted to support the program effort.

PROGRAM STRATEGY (PLAN-OF-WORK)

This phase of program development is concerned with decisions regarding the program strategy. Here the approach to the problems is decided prior to implementation. Decisions are made on the feasibility of allocating resources, and on the best mix of methods and sources for resolving problems.

PURPOSE

The purposes of the "plan-of-work" or "strategy" evaluation are to:

. Determine how resources can be utilized to meet program goals.

. Determine if outside resources are required to meet the objectives.

. Determine the potential costs and benefits of each of several approaches or strategies.

. Determine the mix of resources and methods to reach the program goals and objectives.

. Assess the relevant approaches or strategies which may be appropriate to reach program goals.

. Provide a plan-of-work design needed to accomplish the potential benefits.

. Change activities.

. Identify possible sources of failure.

. Predict whether plan of work will be effective and efficient.

AUDIENCE

The most common audiences for the program strategy or plan-of-work evaluations are program and administrative staff, including Extension staff members, specialists, supervisors, program leaders, administrators, and directors.

Less common audiences are advisory committees, Extension councils, and clientele or special interest groups that cooperate with Extension in planning.

Certain funding bodies and granting agencies may at times be the audience for strategy or plan-of-work evaluations.

ISSUES

The issues in a program strategy evaluation may include
questions such as:

. What educational changes are included in the plan-of-work?

. Are sufficient resources available?

. Is the plan-of-work realistic? Attainable?

. What strategies exist for reaching the goals?

. Is there a better strategy for reaching goals?

. Can a given strategy be translated into an efficient
procedural plan?

. What procedures will be needed to implement a strategy?

. What side effects mignt a particular strategy produce?

. What staff training is required to implement a specific
strategy?

. Is the staffing pattern consistent with needs?

. What budget would be required for the evaluation?

. What is the duration or time frame involved?

. How can existing staff and facilities be used best to
implement a new strategy?

. Were the objectives feasible, legal, and morally
acceptable to the various groups?

. What political support would be needed.

EVIDENCE

Evidence for program strategy or plan-of-work evaluations would
include:

. Descriptions of the environment or program situation,
including objectives or goals, facilities and equipment,
participants, program personnel, procedural design, cost,
budget, and schedule.

. Judgmental evidence, such as statements of appropriate
criteria gathered from programs, personnel, administrators,
potential clientele, councils, and others.

· The quality of the evidence. Is it relevant,
  valid, reliable, objective, unbiased?

DATA GATHERING

To get the necessary information for plan-of-work or strategy
decisions, consider:

. Data sources--who will be able to give evidence?

. Sampling procedures if needed.

. Questions to ask.

. Methods and techniques to use.

ANALYSIS

The analysis of a program strategy or plan-of-work decision
should include:

. Describing program strategies.

. Comparing strategies or potential plans.

. Predicting expected outcomes from each.

. Judging the strategy that is most effective, efficient,
  and appropriate to use in reaching the objectives.

REPORTING

The report will be the plan of work, utilizing the selected
strategy. Decide how this plan of work will be reported to supervisors. In what form? Will it be incorporated into an Extension
reporting system? Will additional written or oral reports need to
be made? How can the report be clarified?

RESOURCES

Resources for program strategy or plan-of-work evaluations are:

. Reports of previous programs.

. Advisory group feedback.

. Extension participant feedback, unsolicited and solicited.

. Reports of programs in other states or agencies.

At times it may be feasible to use consultants and develop new
strategies for plan of work. Volunteers, computers, staff time
and increased financial resources may be needed.

EXAMPLE:* PROGRAM STRATEGY (PLAN-OF-WORK) EVALUATION

4-H Salute to America

During the Bicentennial year, the youth specialist staff in the Lake's Country program planning area organized an extensive program called "4-H Salute to America."

This program was elaborate and time consuming. It included a television program, several separate activities in the counties, and a trip to Europe by some 4-H members.

A decision needed to be made to include similar activities in the ongoing program. Following is a worksheet for this "plan of work" evaluation.

PURPOSE

. Determine the impact of a program that extends beyond county and area boundaries.

. Decide whether it is justifiable to spend staff time on this kind of program.

AUDIENCE

. Area director in Lake's Country area.

. Youth specialists in Lake's Country area.

ISSUES

. Was the Salute to America effort worthwhile?

. What were benefits?

. What were the negative aspects?

. Should a similar program be repeated?

. Is this an appropriate program for Extension?

. Did this program cause a reduction in the regular 4-H program?

. Was the special program worth the time and effort it took?

. Should a similar "beyond the area" program be included as an annual part of the area youth program?

---

*This is an example intended only to illustrate the application of the planning sheet to an actual evaluation effort.

EVIDENCE

Attitudes and feelings of significant people in the Lake's Country area.

DATA GATHERING

. Instrument (attached). (See page 36).

. From whom--selected sample: 4-H members, 4-H leaders, participants in "Salute," nonparticipants in "Salute," 4-H council members and Extension council members.

. Time schedule: Winter 1977.

. Information to be collected by Extension staff services.

ANALYSIS

Relationships and comparisons to be made:

. Responses of participants in "Salute" compared to responses of nonparticipants of "Salute" (4-H members, 4-H Council members, 4-H leaders).

. Responses of Extension council compared to 4-H leaders' responses.

. Statistical analysis to be used--mean and percentage.

. Analysis and interpretation to be done by Extension staff services.

. Conclusion and recommendations to be developed by staff services in consultation with area staff

REPORTING

. Means of presenting the findings: written report to area director.

. Format of the report: Narrative with tables.

. Date for reporting the findings: July 1977.

RESOURCES

. Personnel requirements: minimal.

. Budget: no extra money needed.

    Note: This evaluation was not a report of activities in the
"Salute to America" program, but assessed reactions to determine
the feasibility and acceptability of similar, future programs as
part of the annual youth plan of work in the area.

LAKE'S COUNTRY 4-H STUDY
QUESTIONNAIRE

4-H programs have played an important role in the development
of young people for a number of years. The purpose of this study is to
determine ways in which the 4-H program in Lake's Country could be
more effective. Please answer these questions as best you can from
your own knowledge and feelings.

1. What are the <u>major</u> objectives of 4-H club work? (You may check
   more than one).

   _____ Help boy or girl find a job.
   _____ Educational.
   _____ Earn money.
   _____ Recreational.
   _____ Win awards.
   _____ Social development.
   _____ Learn a trade.
   _____ Earn college scholarship.
   _____ To have fun.
   _____ Develop citizenship responsibilities.
   _____ Other (list) _____.

2. How much have the following activities contributed to the success
   of the 4-H program?

	Much	Some	Little	None
4-H Council				
4-H Demonstration				
4-H Project (subject matter)				
4-H Contests and Awards				
4-H Recreation				
4-H Judging				
4-H Junior Leadership				
4-H Citizenship Short Course				
4-H "Themes" as Salute to America & 4-H, A Family Affair				

3. How much have each of the following activities contributed to increased acquaintanceship and participation of 4-H members beyond
   the local club?

	Much	Some	Little	None
4-H Council				
4-H Committee Assignments				
4-H Junior Leadership				
4-H Judging				
4-H Contests				
4-H State Club Week				
4-H Camping				
4-H "Salute to America"				
Other				

36

4. In your opinion, what do boys and girls you know think of the boys and girls who belong to a 4-H club? (You may check more than one item).

_____ Are interested in learning more about farming.
_____ Are interested in learning things not related to farming.
_____ Are interested in learning more about homemaking.
_____ Are joining a "kids" club.
_____ Will become leaders.
_____ Will have more opportunities for fun.
_____ Will have more opportunities to learn.
_____ Want to win some prize money.
_____ Are lucky.
_____ Something of interest.
_____ Want to learn something that will help them in future life.
_____ Not much else to do.
_____ Wouldn't think much one way or the other.

5. The 4-H Program seeks to work to improve youth. Which of the following statements comes the closest to describing what you consider to be the most important contribution of the 4-H program? (check only one)

_____ 4-H helps the member develop the knowledge needed in adult life.
_____ 4-H helps members interact and work with other people in a cooperative manner for the benefit of all.
_____ The 4-H program helps develop better citizens for the community.
_____ The 4-H program contributes unique learning for the intellectual development of youth.
_____ The 4-H program provides needed services to the communities in which the members live.
_____ The 4-H program develops and teaches skills young people need to grow and develop.

6. What do you consider the main responsibility of your Area Youth Specialist? (check only one)

_____ To work with people who request help.
_____ To work with 4-H members.
_____ To work with 4-H volunteer leaders.
_____ To recruit and train volunteer leaders.
_____ To plan and organize county and area youth events.
_____ To organize and expand new 4-H clubs.
_____ Other (list) _____.

One of the program efforts in the Lake's Country Area was the "4-H Salute to America." This was a special effort in connection with our nation's bicentennial. We would like to ask you a few questions regarding this program.

7. Are you familiar with the program "4-H Salute to America"? ___yes ___no

8. The "4-H Salute to America included many different opportunities for participation in 1975-76. Did you participate in the program? _____ Yes _____ No. If yes, what did you do?

_____

9. What are your feelings about this program? _____

_____

_____

_____

10. In your opinion was "4-H Salute to America": (check one)

_____ An outstanding effort?
_____ A very good program?
_____ All right for those interested?
_____ Of benefit only to a favored few?

11. In your opinion, how did the 4-H Salute to America effect the 4-H program in the Lake's Country Area? (check one)

_____ It included outstanding events that supported the overall 4-H program.
_____ It benefited 4-H in all counties in the area.
_____ It benefited only a select few.
_____ It was more work and time involved than it was worth.
_____ It was detrimental to the 4-H program.

12. Should Extension sponsored programs such as the "4-H Salute to America" which involve effort beyond the boundaries of the area and the county be included annually as a part of the regular youth program? _____ Yes _____ No. Why?

_____

_____

_____

13. A number of youth organizations besides 4-H participated in the bicentennial. Do you remember what they did?

a. Boy Scouts - _____

_____

b. Campfire Girls - _____

_____

38

c. Girl Scouts - _____

_____

d. 4-H - _____

_____

14. What do you think <u>should</u> be the organizational structure of 4-H in the Lake's Country Area?

_____ Area-wide council with representation from all clubs in the area.
_____ County Council with representation from clubs in that county.
_____ Local club autonomy with no county or area council.
_____ Other (describe) _____

15. Following is a list of some things 4-H members say they have gained from various kinds of 4-H experiences.

Place a (+) beside the five items you value <u>most</u> highly. Then place a number beside the items you have marked to indicate the rank of that experience (1=highest.....5=lowest).

Then place a (0) beside the five items you value <u>least</u> highly. Place a number beside these items to indicate your ranking ($\overline{0-1}$ = least, 0-2 = next, ... 0-5 = highest ranking among these five items).

1. ___ Excitement		17. ___ Problem solving ability
2. ___ Close friendship		18. ___ Closer family ties
3. ___ Inner peace		19. ___ Appreciation for nature
4. ___ Sense of self worth		20. ___ Caring for others
5. ___ Ability to make free decisions		21. ___ International understanding
6. ___ Useful physical skills		22. ___ Ability to express myself
7. ___ Public recognition		23. ___ Responsible citizenship
8. ___ Career choice		24. ___ Good ways to use free time
9. ___ Enjoyment and pleasure		25. ___ Increasing independence
10. ___ Approval from others		26. ___ Love
11. ___ Practical knowledge		27. ___ Financial independence
12. ___ Clear personal goals		28. ___ Loyalty from others
13. ___ Creativity		29. ___ Special skills in some areas
14. ___ Flexibility		30. ___ Service to others
15. ___ Rewards for honest efforts		31. ___ Education for parenthood
16. ___ Leadership ability		

I am a/an _____ 4-H Member
_____ 4-H Leader
_____ 4-H Council Member
_____ Extension Council Member

Thank you for helping us with the survey. Check with your local Extension Youth Specialist for a summary of the results.

Name (optional): _____

Address: _____

PROGRAM ACTION (IMPLEMENTATION)

The program action or implementation decision situations occur while a program is in process. Included here are monitoring and other types of decisions needed to keep a program focused on the objectives it was designed to achieve.

PURPOSE:

The purpose of program action or implementation evaluation is to:

. Provide feedback for implementing plans and procedures.

. Identify and monitor potential sources of success and failure.

. Describe what actually takes place.

. Aid in interpreting outcomes.

. Identify and monitor the logistics of the program, communication channels, understanding and acceptance of the program, adequacy of resources, interpersonal relationships, use of staff resources, time schedules, physical facilities, and other things related to the program.

AUDIENCE:

The audience for this kind of evaluation includes groups concerned with the action program, such as:

. Program and administrative staff: Extension staff, specialists, supervisors, program leaders, administrators and directors.

. Clientele groups: Advisory committees and councils, Extension council, clientele organizations, commodity or special interest groups.

. Funding bodies: County boards and courts, state legislature, granting agencies, and Congress.

. Mass media and general public.

ISSUES:

. What changes are being observed in participants?

. Are appropriate techniques of involvement, organization, leadership, and participation used?

40

. Are events occurring as planned?

. Are the strategies being carried out?

. How well are the procedures being carried out?

. What people are being served by the program?

. What kinds of projects show the most success?

. What are the potential sources of failure in the program?

. Are potential sources of failure monitored?

. Are the main features of the project design being carried out?

. Is the administration of funds within legal guidelines?

. Are the current financial and reporting procedures valid?

. Are any significant unanticipated events occurring?

. Is political support being given?

EVIDENCE:

Types of evidence needed will include:

. Movement toward goals, objectives

. Change in participants

. Change in program personnel

. Costs to date

. Conformance to budget

. Adherence to schedule

. Facilities and equipment used

. Specific actions taken

. Balance and scope of the program

. Conformance to Plan-of-Work.

DATA GATHERING:

Considerations for data gathering:

. Determine data sources

. Sampling procedure

. Questions to ask

. Timing of data gathering

. Ethical considerations.

Techniques to consider in data gathering:

. Knowledge and understanding of questions

. Skill or performance ratings

. Attitude scales

. Opinionnaires

. Rating scales

. Interest checks

. Observational techniques

. Adoption of practices.

Methods of collecting data:

. Mailed questionnaires

. Interview (personal, telephone, group)

. Distributed questionnaire or check list

. Tape-recorded interview, discussion or panels

. Systematic observation procedure

. Case study

. Investigative journalism approach.

ANALYSIS:

Analyze the data collected to obtain meaning by comparing:

. Observed processes with intended processes

. Observed impact with intended impact

. Observations for conformance to program plans.

Determine "how-goes-it" from program results, processes and impact.

Compare program data with data from a similar program at this same stage, or compare with an ideal (desired) program.

REPORTING:

Reporting may be of several types:

. Written or oral

. . Technical or nontechnical

. Descriptive or judgmental

. General or specific

. Recommendation-making.

The type will depend on the evidence of the report and the nature of the decisions to be made about the program.

RESOURCES:

The value of feedback information during program action determines the amount of resources in terms of staff time and money that can be devoted to program action evaluation. In most cases it will require staff time, clerical help, and volunteer help to set up a feedback monitoring system.

Radio Services for Print Handicapped

A special program was implemented to provide radio services to
the print handicapped. This program, operated in conjunction with
the Bureau for the Blind, provided receivers to eligible persons.
Extension provided programming over the side-band radio channel
for this audience. Programming included a minimum of three hours
of programs on Monday through Friday including newspaper and
magazine articles and features, books, vocational information
and other items of general interest.

PURPOSE

 . To determine feedback as to programming hours, policies,
  etc.

 . To determine acceptability of the programming presented.

 . To collect suggestions for improving programming.

 . To verify the quality of reception of the radio receivers.

AUDIENCE

 . The program staff of the project.

 . Secondarily--the grantor Bureau for the Blind who
  funded the project.

ISSUES

 . Quality of reception.

 . Broadcasting hours.

 . Usefulness of program content.

 . Help given recipients as a result of the program.

EVIDENCE

The information needed to respond to the issues was obtained
from the recipients of the radio service.

DATA GATHERING

 . Instrument: (attached). (See page 46).

---

*This is an example intended only to illustrate the application of
the planning sheet to an actual evaluation effort.

. From whom: A random sample of recipients of special
side-band receivers.

. Time schedule: January 1977.

. Information to be collected by telephone survey with
interview of those not having telephone.

ANALYSIS

. Responses and comparisons coded and tabulated, using
computer and SPSS computer program.

. Program suggestions from open-ended questions summarized.

. Reactions to various programs summarized.

. Analysis and interpretation done by Extension Studies
and Evaluation Unit.

REPORTING

The findings of the study were prepared in narrative form
for this program committee. This is the basis for preparing an
interim report to the granting agency.

RESOURCES

. Clerical time for a telephone survey.

. Time for tabulations and analysis.

. Some time to interview those having receivers but not
telephones.

RADIO SERVICE FOR PRINT HANDICAPPED
Survey Instrument

Name of Interviewer_____
Respondent's Name_____
Respondent's Address_____
Respondent's Telephone No._____
Calling Hour _____AM/PM _____AM/PM _____AM/PM
      (First)   (Second)   (Third)

    I am calling for the University of Missouri - Columbia Extension. We are
making a study of the special radio service provided for print handicapped.
You were selected from the list of persons supplied the special radio receiver
to be a part of our study. We need your help to make this service more useful
and meaningful for those for whom it is intended. We would appreciate it if
you would answer these questions about our radio and radio programming.

1. How do you rate the quality of reception on your set?

    _____ Excellent   Comments: _____
    _____ Good
    _____ Fair   _____
    _____ Poor
                      _____

2. Is there excessive static, interference or fading in the radio transmission?
    _____ Yes   _____ No.

3. Is the volume control on your receiver adequate for your listening?
    _____ Yes   _____ No.   Comments: _____

    _____

4. How would you rate the quality of the readers on the program?
    _____ Excellent   _____ Good   _____ Fair   _____ Poor.

5. Do reader's mistakes disturb you?   _____ Yes   _____ No.

6. Do you have any favorite readers?   _____ Yes   _____ No.
    If yes, do you remember their names? _____

    _____

7. Do other members of your family listen to the program?
    _____ Yes   _____ No   _____ Sometimes.
    If yes, what is their reaction to the programs? _____

    _____

    _____

8. Do you listen to other programs on the channel, such as - Extension update
    on from 8:00 to 9:00 am or 3:00 to 4:00 pm?   _____Yes   _____No   _____Sometimes.

9. How many hours a day do you listen to the special receiver? _____Hours.

10. How many hours a day do you listen to commercial radio stations? ____Hours.

                                                Time

        Which Stations? _____ _____

                               _____ _____

11. Programs for the print handicapped are broadcast Monday through Friday.
Would weekend broadcasting be desired by you? ____ Yes ____ No.
If yes, what kinds of programs would you like to have on weekends?

_____

_____

_____

_____

12. I will now list some of the program topics we have had on the special radio.
Will you tell me if you remember listening to the program and if you like it
or not?

Time Ref.		Listen				Like	
		Always	Usually	Sometimes	Never	Yes	No
9:00-10:30	Reading from the Columbia Missourian						
	Local News						
	Opinion Page						
	National and International News						
	Sports Page						
	Feature						
	Lighter Side						
10:30-11:00	Radio Reader - A Book						
11:00-11:30	For Your Information:						
Mon.	Opportunities						
Tues.	Leisure & You						
Wed.	Shoppers Guide (Grocery Ads)						
Thurs.	BBC Science Magazine						
Fri.	At Home						
11:30-11:45	Odds and Ends - TV Guide & Anecdotes						
	With Debra Karwoski						
11:45-12:00	KBIA News and Weather						
12:00- 1:00	The Magazine Rack						
Mon.	Current Events - U.S. News & Time						
Tues.	Mainly for Men - Sports Illustrated						
Wed.	Women's Corner - McCalls & Ladies Home Journal						
Thurs.	Consumer News - Money & Changing Times						
Fri.	Neighborhood News - Weekly Newspapers						
1:00- 3:00	Musical Interludes						
2:00- 2:30	Bookshelf						
2:30- 3:00	Spider's Web						
4:00- 4:55	Reading from Jefferson City Capital News						
	Local and National News						
	Opinion Page - Editorial Page						
	Sports						
	Features						

13. Have you been helped by these programs? ____ Yes ____ No.

    If yes, how? _____

_____

14. Do you use any other services especially for the print handicapped?
    ____ Yes ____ No. If yes, which ones (e.g. Wolfner Library Services)?

_____

_____

15. Do you have any suggestions to make regarding the programming?

_____

_____

_____

_____

16. Would you give us some information?

    Number of adults and children in your home: ____ adults ____ children.

17. Are you ____ married ____ single ____ widowed ____ separated?

18. We would like to send you program guide information.

    Can you read large type? ____ Yes ____ No.

    Do you read Braille? ____ Yes ____ No.

    Would you like to get this information on a cassette tape? ____Yes ____No.

    Do you have a cassette tape player? ____ Yes ____ No.

PROGRAM PRODUCT EVALUATION (ACCOMPLISHMENTS)

This kind of evaluation determines the impact of an Extension program (after it is completed). Decisions from the product evaluation will determine whether to expand, continue, modify, or terminate a program.

PURPOSE

The purpose of product evaluation is to:

. Identify the results and value of a program.

. Determine the extent to which objectives have been or are being attained.

. Compare outcomes with the objectives of the program.

. Decide whether to continue, modify, expand, or end the program.

. Relate the results of situation, plan-of-work, and/or program action evaluations in order to measure and interpret outcomes.

AUDIENCE

The audience of product evaluation consists of:

Clientele Groups

. Advisory committees and councils

. Extension councils

. Clientele organizations

. Commodity or special interest groups

. Clientele of Extension

Program and Administrative Staff

. Extension staff members

. Extension specialists

. Extension supervisors

. Program leaders

. Administrators

. Directors

Appropriating Bodies

. County boards or courts

. State legislatures

. Granting agencies

. Congress

General Public

. Press

. Radio

. Television

ISSUES

Issues or questions about program outcomes are as follows:

. What changes have occurred in the participants?

. Were clientele needs met?

. Have the program objectives been reached?

. Was staff morale maintained?

. What (if any) side effects occurred as a result of the program?

. What happened that would not have happened without the program?

. Was the expense of the program worthwhile?

. What were the costs of one program compared with another?

. Are program funders getting their money's worth?

. What are the major complaints or faults about the program?

. What are the evident short-range positive aspects of the program, as well as "spin-off" or anticipated long-range benefits of the program?

. How well were absolute standards met?

. What value do these changes have?

EVIDENCE

The kind of evidence needed will depend on the issues or questions to be addressed in the evaluation. It includes descriptive evidence such as:

. Situation

. Inputs or plan of work

. Goals, objectives

. Facilities and equipment used

. Participants

. Program personnel

. Procedures and program design used

. Costs

. Budget

. Schedule

. Outcome or changes created.

Evidence collected should have quality. Measures of quality are:

. Relevance relates to issues under consideration

. Validity measures what it is supposed to measure

. Reliability: consistent in its measurement

. Objectivity

. Determination of biases or possible biases

. Balance and scope

. Credibility of the evaluator.

DATA GATHERING

Data gathering is collecting the evidence to be used to resolve the issues so that the purposes of the evaluation may be attained.

Factors to consider in data gathering are:

. Determining data sources: Who has the answers you need?

. Sampling procedures

. Timing of data gathering

. Knowing what questions to ask

: Ethical considerations

. Planning treatment of data.

Techniques to consider in data gathering include:

. Attitude scales

. Skill or performance ratings

. Opinionnaires

. Rating scales

. Interest check

. Observational techniques.

Methods of collecting data:

. Mailed questionnaires

. Interview (personal, telephone, or group)

. Distributed questionnaire or checklist

. Tape-recorded interview, discussion or panels

. Case study

. Investigative journalism.

ANALYSIS

The data are analyzed by making comparisons that show relevant facets of the program.

Compare:

. Observed evidence (outcomes) with anticipated outcomes

. Observed audience(outcomes) with results of similar programs

. Program impact with reduction of needs or problems.

<u>Decide</u>:

Make decisions and judgments about the issues on the basis of evidence so that the concern of the audience will be answered and the purpose of the evaluation achieved.

REPORTING

The product or outcome evaluation report may be:

. Written or oral

. Technical or nontechnical

. Descriptive or judgmental

. General or specific

. In the form of recommendations.

The type of the report will depend upon the issues, audience, and the comprehensiveness of the program. It may be:

. A case study

. Illustrated with graphs and charts

. In question-answer format

. A product display

. In multimedia (slide-tape) form

. Executive summary

. Journalistic.

RESOURCES

The resources for an outcome evaluation may consist of:

. Data from existing records

. Census and census-type data

. Reports and records from similar programs

. Program report

. SEMIS data

. Community surveys

. Information from participants.

Special resources for the evaluation include clerical and staff time, money for data collection, analysis and interpretation, as well as administrative support.

EXAMPLE:* <u>PROGRAM PRODUCT EVALUATION</u>

Evaluation of National EFNEP Workshop

PURPOSE

   . To determine if the objectives of the workshop were achieved.

   . To demonstrate to ECOP subcommittee the workshop was worth
     the time and expense.

AUDIENCE

   The ECOP subcommittee and program planning committee.

ISSUES

   . Were <u>EFNEP Guidelines</u> adequately presented and understood?

   . Were the selected subjects for treatment meaningful to
     participants?

   . Were those attending given an adequate opportunity to
     participate?

   . Were their needs and concerns regarding EFNEP met?

   . How are the materials presented to be used in the state?

   . What was the outcome of such use?

EVIDENCE

   Evidence to be collected in three phases:

   . At end of workshop session

   . As planned changes resulting from workshop (2 weeks after
     workshop)

   . Report of changes made as a result of workshop (July 1, 1977).

DATA GATHERING

   . Instrument   (See page 57).

   . Sampling: 100 percent of workshop attendees report from
     each state on plans and on changes made.

---

*This is an example intended only to illustrate the application
of the planning sheet to an actual evaluation effort.

. Time schedule: End of Workshop Report (October 30, 1976)
                  Report of Plans (November 15, 1976)
                  Report of Changes Made (July 31, 1977)

. Information collected: End of Workshop Survey--John Gross,
                          Missouri
                          Survey of Plans--Nancy B. Leidenfrost,
                          ES-USDA
                          Survey of Changes Made--Nancy B.
                          Leidenfrost, ES-USDA

ANALYSIS

Information from end of workshop reports was coded and summarized
by computer. Data was coded and entered into the computer using SPSS
computer program.

Analysis of reaction was compared by position in EFNEP and work
area in EFNEP. Open-ended questions were summarized separately.

Summary and recommendations were made by the person collecting
the information.

REPORTING

A written report showing tables of responses and narrative
interpretation was prepared for the program planning committee and
ECOP Subcommittee representatives.

A summary of plans and reports of changes too will be prepared
later.

RESOURCES

The program planning committee provided staff resources needed.
Routine clerical work was minimal and was performed by the staff
secretary.

1. What is your position in EFNEP?

_____ EFNEP State Coordinator   _____ State Home Economics Program Leader
_____ Food and Nutrition Specialist   _____ District or Area Supervisor
_____ State 4-H Leader or Specialist   _____ Other (Specify) _____

2. Is your work in EFNEP with:

_____ Adults Only   _____ Adults & Youth   _____ Youth Only

3. Please rate the following program segments as you felt they dealt with your concerns:

	Not Applicable	Excellent	Good	Fair	Needed Improvement
Program Guidelines					
Non-Program Families					
Food Recalls					
Quality Programming/Youth					
Progression Model					
Legal Aspects					
Nutrition Change in Disadvantaged Youth (N.C. Study)					
Program Visibility					
Program Development Groups					
EFNEP - The Team Approach					
Volunteer Materials					
Nutrition Lessons					

4. What other concerns did you have that were not covered by the workshop?

_____

_____

_____

5. Rate the following as perceived by you:

	Excellent	Good	Fair	Poor
Group Discussions				
Exhibits				
Audio Visual Demonstrations				
Breaks and Free Time				
Dinner Theater				
Meals and Food				
Meeting Rooms and Facilities				
Opportunity for Involvement (Workshops)				

6. As far as you were concerned, what was the most valuable part of the workshop?

_____

_____

7. How could the workshop have been improved? _____
   _____
   _____

8. How often should national workshops be conducted? _____
   _____

9. Overall, to what extent do you think the stated objectives of the conference were reached?

   _____ Almost all objectives were reached completely.
   _____ Most objectives were reached adequately.
   _____ Some objectives were reached and some were not.
   _____ Objectives were reached only to a limited extent.
   _____ Objectives were not reached.

10. Compared with other workshops you have attended, do you feel you have profited from this one:

    _____ More   _____ About the Same   _____ Less

    Comments: _____
    _____
    _____

11. Rate the usability of materials presented at the workshop: (Check on line)

	Excellent Very Usable		Of Some Use		Not Usable For Us
a. New Guidelines					
b. Youth Evaluation Model					
c. Progression Model					
d. Volunteer Materials					
e. Nutrition Lessons					

12. Add any other comments regarding the workshop: _____
    _____
    _____
    _____

NATIONAL EFNEP WORKSHOP EVALUATION - 1976

State _____

1. What specific changes do you intend to implement as a result of this workshop?

Guidelines and Policies: _____

_____ _____

_____

_____

4-H EFNEP Programs (Including Evaluation of 4-H EFNEP): _____

_____ _____

_____

_____

Progression Model: _____

_____ _____

_____

_____

Nutrition Lessons: _____

_____ _____

_____

_____

The Team Approach: _____

_____ _____

_____

_____

Program Development Groups: _____

_____ _____

_____

_____

Publicity and Program Visibility: _____ Estimated Date

_____ _____

_____

_____

Volunteers: _____

_____ _____

_____

_____

Legal Aspects Relevant to EFNEP: _____

_____ _____

_____

_____

Use of Food Recall Records: _____

_____ _____

_____

_____

Non-Program Families: _____

_____ _____

_____

_____

Other (Specify): _____

_____ _____

_____

_____

Mail to: Nancy Leidenfrost
          Deputy Asst. Administrator - EFNEP
          Extension Service - USDA
          Washington, D. C. 20250

By: October 19, 1976

REFERENCES*

Type or Category of Evaluation:

Stufflebeam, Daniel L. et.al. Educational Evaluation and Decision
Making. F. E. Peacock, Inc., Itasca, Illinois, 1971. pp. 218-
235.

Stufflebeam, Daniel L. "Toward A Science of Educational Evaluation"
Educational Technology, July 30, 1968. pp. 5-12.

Raudabaugh, J. Neil. "Evaluation As A Concept," Extension Service,
U. S. Department of Agriculture, Washington, D. C., Mimeographed.
16 pp. (1-75).

Worthen, Blaine R. and James R. Sanders. Educational Evaluation:
Theory and Practice. Charles A. Jones Publishing Co., Worthington, Ohio 1972. pp. 22-26.

Purpose:

Matthews, Joseph L. "The Place of Evaluation in Extension" in Byrn,
Darcie (Ed.) Evaluation in Extension. H. M. Ives and Son,
Topeka, Kansas, 1967. pp. 10-12.

Raudabaugh, J. Neil. "Evaluation As A Concept," Extension Service,
U. S. Department of Agriculture, Washington, D. C., Mimeographed.
16 pp. (1-75).

Frutchey, Fred P. "Extension Evaluation," Extension Service, U. S.
Department of Agriculture, Mimeographed. (10-54).

Grotelueschen, Arden, et.al. An Evaluation Planner. University of
Illinois, Urbana, Illinois, 1974.

Steele, Sara M. Contemporary Approaches to Program Evaluation.
ERIC Clearinghouse on Adult Education, Syracuse, New York, 1973.
p. 29.

Suchman, Edward. Evaluative Research. Russell Sage Foundation,
New York, 1967. p. 141.

Audience:

Worthen, Blaine R. and James R. Sanders. Educational Evaluation:
Theory and Practice. Charles A. Jones Publishing Co., Worthington, Ohio, 1972. p. 200.

─────────────
*Additional references such as questionnaire aids and a catalog
of evaluation instruments are in the planning process,

Fessenden, Mrs. Jewell C. and Ward F. Porter. "Preparing A
Research or Study Report" in Byrn, Darcie (Ed). Evaluation
in Extension. H. M. Ives and Sons, Topeka, Kansas, 1968.
p. 83.

Frutchey, Fred P. "Extension Evaluation" Extension Service, U. S.
Department of Agriculture, Washington, D. C. Mimeographed.
(10-54).

Grotelueschen, Arden, et.al. An Evaluation Planner. University
of Illinois, Urbana, Illinois, 1974.

Issues:

Porter, Ward F. "Identifying Problem Areas and Study Objectives"
in Byrn, Darcie (Ed.). Evaluation in Extension. H. M. Ives
and Sons, Topeka, Kansas, 1967. pp. 30-32.

Frutchey, Fred P. "Extension Evaluation" Extension Service, U. S.
Department of Agriculture, Washington, D. C. Mimeographed.
(10-54).

Raudabaugh, J. Neil. "Evaluation As A Concept" Extension Service,
U. S. Department of Agriculture, Washington, D. C. Mimeographed.
(1-75).

Grotelueschen, Arden, et.al. An Evaluation Planner. University of
Illinois, Urbana, Illinois, 1974.

Bennett, Claude F. "Analyzing Impacts of Extension Programs" U. S.
Department of Agriculture, Washington, D. C., April 1976.

Evidence:

Sabrosky, Mrs. Laurel K. "Evidence of Progress Toward Objectives"
in Byrn, Darcie (Ed.). Evaluation in Extension. H. M. Ives
and Sons, Topeka, Kansas, 1967. pp. 25-29.

Frutchey, Fred P. "Extension Evaluation" Extension Service, U. S.
Department of Agriculture, Washington, D. C. Mimeographed.
(10-54).

Grotelueschen, Arden, et.al. An Evaluation Planner. University of
Illinois, Urbana, Illinois, 1974.

Bennett, Claude F. "Analyzing Impacts of Extension Programs" U. S.
Department of Agriculture, Washington, D. C., April 1976.

Data Gathering:

Baumel, C. Phillip, Daryl J. Hobb, and Ronald C. Powers. The Community Survey. Iowa State University, Ames, Iowa, 1964. pp. 5-18.

Berdie, Douglas and John F. Anderson. "Questionnaire: Design and Use." The Scarecrow Press, Inc., Metuchen, N.J., 1974.

Borich, Gary D. (Ed.). "Evaluating Educational Programs and Products." Educational Technology Publications, Englewood Cliffs, N.J., May 1974. pp. 289-293.

Steele, Sara M. "Developing A Questionnaire." University of Wisconsin, Extension Division of Program and Staff Development, Madison, Wisconsin, 1974.

Gallup, Gladys. "Devices for Collecting Data" and "Construction of an Evaluation Device" in Byrn, Darcie (Ed.). Evaluation in Extension. H. M. Ives and Sons, Topeka, Kansas, 1968. pp. 57-69.

Grotelueschen, Arden, et.al. An Evaluation Planner. University of Illinois, Urbana, Illinois, 1974.

Sabrosky, Mrs. Laurel K. "Sampling" in Byrn, Darcie (Ed.). Evaluation in Extension. H. M. Ives and Sons, Topeka, Kansas, 1968. pp. 37-44.

Frutchey, Fred P. "Extension Evaluation." Extension Service, U. S. Department of Agriculture, Washington, D. C. Mimeographed. (10-54).

Oppenheim, A. N. Questionnaire Design and Attitude Measurement. Basic Books, Inc., New York, 1966.

Gallup, George. A Guide to Public Opinion Polls. Princeton, 1948. pp. 40-41.

Payne, Stanley L. The Art of Asking Questions. Princeton, 1951. pp. 151-157.

Van Dalen, Debold B. Understanding Educational Research. McGraw-Hill Book Company, New York, 1962. pp. 372-373.

Snedecor, G. W. Statistical Methods. Iowa State Press, Ames, Iowa, 1956. pp. 501-505.

Kish, Leslie. Survey Sampling. John Wiley and Sons. New York, 1965. pp. 18-24.

Analysis:

Frutchey, Fred P. 'Extension Evaluation." Extension Service, U. S. Department of Agriculture, Washington, D. C. Mimeographed. (10-54).

Bennett, Claude F. "Analyzing the Impacts of Extension Programs." U. S. Department of Agriculture, Washington, D. C., April 1976.

Porter, Ward F. and Mrs. Jewell Fessenden. "Tabulation" and
"Analysis and Interpretation" in Byrn, Darcie (Ed.). Evaluation in Extension. H. M. Ives and Sons, Topeka, Kansas,
1968. pp. 70-82.

Steele, Sara M. Contemporary Approaches to Program Evaluation.
ERIC Clearinghouse on Adult Education, Syracuse, New York,
1973.

Neidt, C. O. "Evaluation Reports." Colorado State University,
Fort Collins, Colorado, 1969. Mimeographed.

Grotelueschen, Arden, et.al. An Evaluation Planner. University
of Illinois, Urbana, Illinois, 1974.

Reporting:

Fessenden, Mrs. Jewell G. and Ward F. Porter. "Preparing A Research
Study Report" in Byrn, Darcie (Ed.). Evaluation in Extension.

Grotelueschen, Arden, et.al. An Evaluation Planner. University
of Illinois, Urbana, Illinois, 1974.

Stake, Robert E. "Evaluation Design, Instrumentation, Data Collec-
tion, and Analysis of Data" in Worthen, Blaine and Sanders,
Educational Evaluation: Theory and Practice. Charles A. Jones
Publishing Co., Worthington, Ohio, 1973. pp. 303-316.

Stufflebeam, Daniel L., et.al. Educational Evaluation and Decision
Making. F. E. Peacock Publishers, Inc. Itasca, Illinois, 1971.
pp. 168, 197-213.

GLOSSARY OF EVALUATION TERMS**

Accountability -- The responsibility for developing, evaluating, and measuring effective performance of programs in an organization on a continuing basis. Being responsible for making actions open to view; keeping records and disclosing the activities and results of a program.

Aggregation -- Assembling data into groups or classes for reports and other purposes.

Analysis, data** -- Purposeful ordering of data in a manner that facilitates objective interpretation with respect to a particular question, concern, problem, or objective.

Audience* -- That aggregate of participants who are actual or potential program clientele.

Bias -- Error of the estimate from the true proportion that exists in a population.

Case Study -- A study of one or a few individual cases reporting the chronology of the development of a project or activity or a story of an individual family.

Coordination* -- A condition in which efforts are joined into common action toward defined objectives with each person, organization, agency, and/or department knowing his (or their) function and role in relation to that of others involved.

Criteria* -- Standards for judging; standards or norms selected as a basis for use in making quantitative or qualitative comparisons, judgments, or evaluations. Qualities or dimensions on which a program, product, or activity is to be judged.

Decision -- A choice among alternatives. A conclusion arrived at after consideration.

Decision Situation -- A set of alternatives for consideration.

Development -- The process of research planning, implementation, and evaluation.

Education* -- The process of bringing about changes in people, i.e., interests, desires, understandings, attitudes, knowledges, skills, abilities, and practices.

* Taken from Extension Program Development, by Program Development Ad Hoc Committee, Roger Lawrence, Chairman, 1973. pp. 14-16.
** This glossary includes the terms commonly used in the area of evaluation. Not all of the terms are referred to in the Planner.

Evaluation -- A process, with many forms and a variety of purposes.
Evaluation must take into account a variety of audiences or
publics. The essential components of evaluation are criteria,
evidence, and judgment.

-- Context Evaluation (situation) -- Provides the rationale
for determining objectives and setting priorities. It
defines the relevant environment, describes the desired
and actual conditions pertaining to the environment and
identifies unmet needs and unused opportunities.

-- Input Evaluation (plan of work) -- Provides information
for determining how to use resources to meet program
goals. It involves identifying and assessing (1) relevant capabilities for achieving program goals;
(2) strategies for achieving program goals; (3) designs
for implementing a strategy.

-- Implementation Evaluation (program action) -- Provides
feedback. It detects or predicts defects in the
procedural design and its implementation provides
information for decisions that are a part of
implementation, and maintains a record of the
procedures followed.

-- Formative Evaluation -- Evaluation used to facilitate
decisions as the program progresses. Its primary
concern is program improvement.

-- Product Evaluation (outcome) -- Measures and interprets
attainments during and at the end of the program.
It's concerned with main effects, side effects,
costs, and superiority.

-- Summative Evaluation -- End of program evaluation which
is concerned with determining overall program
effectiveness.

-- Impact evaluation (product) -- Evaluation that is concerned with the purpose or significance of activities.
It deals with the consequences of projects, program
components, and other activities that are planned or
unplanned.

Evidence -- Any information which may contribute to the consideration
of a particular issue and is based on objective criteria.

Information -- Descriptive or interpretative data about entities
(tangible or intangible) and their relationship in terms of
some purpose.

Interview Schedule -- List of items or questions, together with
specific instructions for the interview, to be used in
gathering data by the interview method.

-- Telephone Interview Schedule -- The series of items to
be used for gathering information from respondents
by use of the telephone. Include specific
instructions for the interviewer.

-- Individual Interview Schedule -- Information collected
by an interviewer from a subject on a one-to-one
basis. The interview may be structured (interview
schedule) or unstructured (interviewer asks
questions based on written or mental notes).

-- Group Interview -- Prospective respondents are assembled
in a group. Each person in the group is asked to
record his/her answer as questions are read to them.

Issues -- The central concerns of an evaluation; those questions to
be addressed by the evaluation (e.g., accomplishment of goals,
effectiveness of programs, etc.).

Judging -- It is the act of choosing among several decision
alternatives, hence, the act of decisionmaking.

Learning* -- The change in behavior of a person that takes place
as a result of stimuli and the individual's reaction to them.

Learning Experience* -- The interaction between the learner and
conditions in the environment to which the individual
reacts; the encounter through which learning takes place
and educational objectives are attained.

Macroscopic Level -- An evaluator's point of reference focused on
overall evaluation of a total system.

Microscopic Level -- An evaluator's point of reference focused on
detailed evaluation of specific elements in a total system.

Method* -- A planned procedure, sequence of experiences, activities,
or events designed to bring about a desired end.

Mission* -- A statement of the broad role or function of the Extension
Service which serves as a guide to the organization and facilitates understanding on the part of Extension publics.

Objective* -- A goal, end, or aim stated in regard to a concern,
problem, or subject.

-- Attainable Objective -- An objective that can be reached
by the recipients considering the resources available
to be used.

-- Educational Objective* -- A statement that specifies the
learner (audience), the desired behavior, and the
content or area of life in which the behavior is to
operate.

67

-- Measurable Objective -- A statement of program intent that
can, with a degree of certainty, be accurately described
when attained. Measurability would include quantitative
and/or qualitative descriptive units related to
determining results, outcomes, or effectiveness of
the objectives. To be measurable, the objective
must have some chance of being implemented (opera-
tionalized) and attained.

-- Operational Objective* -- A statement of procedure to
be undertaken; a step or unit of what is to be done.

-- Organizational Objective* -- A statement of change to
be accomplished in the development or maintenance
of an organization; a statement of a goal, end,
or aim of a group, social entity, or functional
structure of people.

-- Plan-of-Work Objective* -- A statement of specific
change to be accomplished in a given time period
through planned activity and based on program
level objective.

-- Program Objective* -- A statement of change to be
accomplished within a designated period of time
(a year or longer).

-- Societal Objective* -- A statement of change desired
in regard to the broad human, social, economic,
or institutional concerns of people.

-- Teaching Level Objective* -- A statement which
specifies under what conditions and to what
extent a specific kind of learner performance
(behavioral change) is expected relative to
a program and plan-of-work objective.

Plan-of-Work (written document)* -- A written outline of strategy
for one year or less for each problem or concern included in
a program that sets forth in an integrated and coordinated
manner the following elements: (1) educational operations
and organizational objectives to be achieved; (2) learning
experiences, activities, events, and/or situations to be
undertaken, calendarized, and related to appropriate
objectives; (3) evidence of accomplishment, and calendar
for evaluation; (4) time to be devoted to each activity,
event, and/or learning situation; (5) who will assume
primary and support leadership responsibilities; and
(6) coordination, internal and external.

Problem or Need (educational)* -- A situation or condition which,
after study, is believed should be changed and the desired

change can be brought about in total or in part through educational endeavor; the set of conditions that prevents change from "what is" to "what ought to be."

Process* -- A course of action, procedure or a series of steps leading toward an end.

Program -- A series of planned events (or activities) with specific objectives. These planned events are designed to deliver educational information for the purpose or purposes expressed in the objective(s). Under the concept of program there are a number of "activities" conducted to reach the program objective(s). These "activities" are time-structured or sequenced to take advantage of conditions that facilitate learning or acceptance of the information being provided. Program is not considered to be synonomous with "activity." Activities are the various components or planned events that contribute to the achievement of the program objectives.

Program Accomplishments -- Intended and unintended results of program activity.

Program Development (programming, progarm management)* -- The continuous series of processes which includes organizing, planning a program, preparing a plan-of-work and teaching plans, implementing the plans, evaluating, and reporting accomplishments.

Program, Extension* -- Agreed-upon priority needs, concerns, problems, and interests that fall within the scope of the Extension units' responsibilities, together with the relevant objectives that are to be achieved within a designated period of time.

Program Evaluation* -- The process by which evidence or data, objectives, and/or criteria are used as a basis for judgment in determining accomplishments in a program.

Program Planning (program determination)* -- The process by which people, usually by means of a committee(s) or council(s), Extension personnel and other resource persons, determine a program.

Questionnaire -- A schedule of questions used to gather data for a study or research project.

Research - Studious inquiry or critical and exhaustive investigation having as its aim new and generalizable knowledge.

-- Evaluative Research -- A specialized kind or branch of research that deals with valuing. (Compare with evaluation)

<u>Reliability</u> -- The consistency of responses obtained from similar
subjects at different times.

<u>Sampling</u> -- Taking a small representative collection from some
larger population about which we wish information. The
sample is examined and the facts about it learned.

-- Random Sampling -- Selecting a sample in such a way
that each item or person in the population being
studied will have an equal chance to be selected
for the study.

-- Stratified Random Sampling -- Dividing the population
to be studied into subgroups and sampling each
subgroup randomly. This procedure insures that
each subgroup will be adequately represented in
the final sample.

<u>Systematic Observation</u> -- Practices which have been recommended
for an area observed and recorded in some systematic manner.

<u>Teaching</u> -- The guidance of the activities of the learner: the
stimulation of desired activities and the providing of
educative experience that will result in desired behavior
changes on the part of the learner.

<u>Teaching Plan</u>* -- A detailed outline, based on an educational
objective set forth in a plan of work, that states the
specific teaching level objectives in terms of the
learner's needs, the subject matter to be taught, the
educational techniques, aids, and materials to be
used, and standards and procedures for evaluation.

<u>Validity</u> -- The degree to which data gathering instrument
measures the objective it is supposed to measure.

TABLE I
PROGRAM DEVELOPMENT – EVALUATION – DECISION MAKING*
Summary of Relationships

Program Development Component	Category of Evaluation To Conduct	Decision Situation

Situational Analysis:
 	
Basis for Program Planning Determination of Situation:
 	
Concerns..Problems Interests....Needs
 	
To make and record decisions with regard to priority problems and objectives to be included in the planning unit's (Extension's) program.
	Program Determination (Situation) Evaluation:
	
	A. Serves decision making for planning new and on-going programs.
	
	B. Diagnostic in nature; i.e. attempts to determine difference between the intended objectives and the actual program outcomes.
	
	C. Provides information for planning the program:
	
	  1. To conform to current needs.
	  2. To meet changing needs.
		Program Planning Decisions:
		
		A. Planning decisions relative to:
		
		  1. Program goals.
		  2. Needs of target groups to be served.
		  3. Program objectives.
		
		B. Planning decisions that will produce a (greater) correspondence between intended and actual outcomes; i.e. reformulation of program plans.
		
		C. Planning decisions relative to utilizing evaluation results for program;
		
		  1. Improvement.
		  2. Modification.
		  3. Continuation.
		  4. Termination.

*Developed by E. Richard Wheaton, Program & Staff Development, Extension Service, U.S.D.A.

TABLE I
PROGRAM DEVELOPMENT – EVALUATION – DECISION MAKING*
Summary of Relationships

Program Development Component	Category of Evaluation To Conduct	Decision Situation
Development of Program Plans:	**Program Strategy (Plan-of-Work) Evaluation:**	**Structuring or Strategy Decisions:**
Strategies for Program Action The utilization of information and data for development of plans of work that include priority problems and objectives of educational programs.	A. Serves decision making; i.e., concerned with making previously identified & clarified program goals operational. B. Descriptive in nature; i.e., it describes the resources available and determines the best use of resources for the development of a plan(s) to meet intended goals. C. Provides information about how resources are to be utilized; who is responsible for what and when, and intended effects the program will have on the target group.	A. Strategy decisions relative to action planned and undertaken to accomplish program objectives. B. Strategy decisions that provide an assessment of how resources have been or will be utilized. The results of the assessment are decisions for implementing a program or recommendations for redesigning an ongoing program. C. Strategy decisions relative to utilizing evaluation results about strategies to: 1. Accomplish objectives. 2. Effectively utilize staff and resources. 3. Schedule program activities. 4. Assess cost of program strategies. 5. Determine alternative solutions and decide which were or will be most practical and effective.

Issued December 1977.